Echoes of th

C000077598

Events, People & Places in the 1960s in & around the Derby

Ron Duggins

Landmark Publishing

Published by

Ashbourne Hall, Cokayne Ave
Ashbourne, Derbyshire DE6 1EJ England
Tel: (01335) 347349 Fax: (01335) 347303
e-mail: landmark@clara.net
web site: www.landmarkpublishing.co.uk

ISBN 13: 978-1-84306-346-9

© Ron Duggins 2007

British Library Cataloguing in Publication Data: a catalogue
record for this book is available from the British Library.

Printed by Cromwell Press Ltd, Trowbridge
Designed by Michelle Hunt

Front Cover: John Turner School pupils sit this one out at Four Lanes End, Darley Dale.

Back Cover Top: Excited youngsters from local schools crowd the pavements on Dale Road in Matlock hoping to catch a glimpse of the Royal visitor.

Back cover Middle Left: Once a year Youlgrave residents dammed the river in Bradford Dale for an aquatic pillow fight which generally was fun for the winner but left the losers with dampened spirits.

Back cover Middle Right: Matlock Round Table found a novel way of advertising their charity stall at the show with these bikini-clad young ladies. Sisters Joan and Angela Noble flank former Miss Matlock and later top model Barbara Dick.

Back cover bottom: A trio of Old Bailean rugby players whose service to the club added up to nearly 70 years. On the left are John Hooton (36), centre is Haydn Kingman (44), right is Sid Quigley, vice-chairman.

Page 3: Platts Motors Garage on Causeway Lane in Matlock one day in 1968.

Echoes of the Dales

Events, People & Places in the 1960s in & around the Derbyshire Dales

Ron Duggins

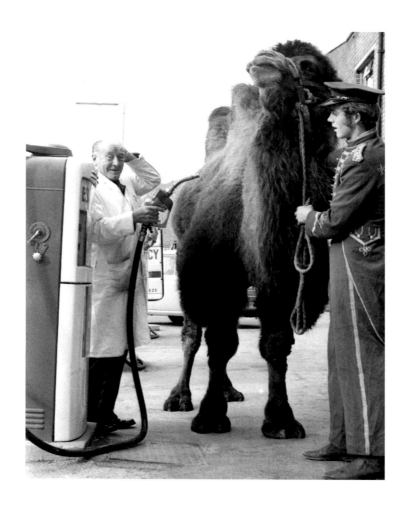

Landmark Publishing

There's a saying that printers' ink is in your blood, and that the smell of newsprint stays with you forever. My father Herbert Duggins (above) was a time-served printer of the old school when type had to be painstakingly and meticulously set by hand. He would meet the customer, set the type, cut the paper, print the job, trim it and finally package it ready for collection. Before the war he worked for Derbyshire and Smith in Matlock and after that for Frank Roberts in tiny premises in Crown Square. He was later 'poached' by Smith's Printing Works and the Coming Events on Bakewell Road with the promise of going away to learn how to operate a new machine which would revolutionise printing in Matlock. Called an Intertype, the machine did away with hand-setting, my father sat at a keyboard and produced as much type in an hour as could have been produced in a day. To see his fingers glide over the keys was magic and as a youngster I watched him in absolute awe. Gosh I wish I could do that. But father was adamant that I should not follow in his footsteps, but go to art college. So one day after he had gone to work I secretly called to see Herbert Smith, the MD, got a job and after lunch we rode our bicycles back to Matlock, but instead of going on to school turned in with him. "Where are you going?" The rest is history. So this book is a dedication to my father for all his teaching and inspiration, to my mother Lucy for seeing that we went to work properly fed, to my brother Adrian who eventually joined us and finally to everyone who ever worked at the printing works and *Matlock Mercury*. We were a happy bunch of amateurs doing a professional job!

Ron Duggins

The Queen visited Matlock and district in May, 1968. While it brought a great deal of happiness to hundreds of people, one man who had good reason to feel unhappy was Station Master Alan Fletcher who, only a few weeks earlier was retired and replaced for the occasion by the British Railways Area Manager. Pictured on Matlock Station platform is Lord Lieutenant Sir Ian Walker Okeover introducing the Queen to town council chairman Councillor Harry Walters and his wife. Also pictured are Mrs James Scott-Hopkins, wife of the West Derbyshire MP, and Mr Walter Stansfield, MC, Chief Constable of Derby County and Borough Constabulary.

Excited youngsters from local schools crowd the pavements on Dale Road in Matlock hoping to catch a glimpse of the Royal visitor as she passed on her way to Lea Green Sports and Training Centre.

Signing the visitors book watched by Mr Peter Townend, Principal of the Centre, Councillor Norman Wilson, chairman of Derbyshire County Council, and Mrs Jan Wilson, and Mrs Trippett, wife of Alderman J W Trippett.

A big moment at Lea Mills for 11-year-old Carole Bush who was chosen to present the Royal bouquet, under the watchful eyes of Mr Ian Maclean, chairman of John Smedley Ltd and the Countess of Cromer, Lady-in-Waiting.

Miss Elsie Gaunt demonstrates draw-threading to the Queen, watched by Managing Director Mr W T Holder.

Getting a closer look at some of the finer garments that were helping to boost the Company's export trade.

No flagging spirits for these youngsters patiently waiting in the gym at Lea Green.

Holloway Dramatic Society set themselves a huge task in 1964 when they performed 'She passed through Lorraine' in the village hall. It was set in feudal France during the 15th century, and takes a light-hearted look at Joan of Arc as she passed through the town. Jenny Bush played the lead role, ably supported by Steven Walker, Janet Worthy, Roger Worthy, Alice Knowles, Marion Keene, Reg Wallace, Howard Davidson, Michael Braithwaite, Alan Worthy and Betty Thompson. Producer was Fran Higton and the play was written by Lionel Hale.

When the railway sidings closed at Northwood, Bill Salt became a council lengthsman in Darley Dale. He could be seen sweeping the paths and kerbs, occasionally stopping for a chat with passers-by. One very warm day, he recalled later, while working on the A6 he felt a burning sensation on his feet and legs. Looking down he saw his shoes were on fire. He fell to the ground and rolled about in agony while trying to douse the flames. Luckily for him, a passing council lorry pulled up and the driver and his mate "put him out" to quote Bill's own words.

Apparently Bill kept his working boots in a shed where highly combustible weed-killer was stored and this had impregnated them. How they came to be ignited is still a mystery, but perhaps the fact that he was ever more known as Hot Foot Billy could be a clue.

Big names in the world of cinema arrived in the area in 1968 when Ken Russell brought his director's talents and stars to film 'Women in Love'. The original book was written by D H Lawrence and explores the relationships, personalities and philosophies of two men and women in the high society of the early 1900s. Stars including Alan Bates, Oliver Reed, Glenda Jackson, Jennie Linden and Eleanor Bron all had key roles in this 90-minute film. Pictured (top left) outside St Giles' Church, Matlock Town, where the wedding scenes were shot are Alan Bates (Rupert Birkin) and coachmen Laurie Dale and Peter Kay, who along with the coach and horses were from the Red House Stables at Darley Dale.

Above: A close encounter with Jennie Linden...locals Mrs Peggy Watson and Mrs Phyllis Hunt join others on Church Street.

Right: Jennie Linden (Ursula Brangwen) makes a last-minute adjustment to her head-dress.

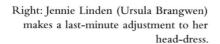

Oliver Reed as
Gerald Crich.

A man with a lot on his mind – Director Ken Russell. He received a lot of complaints about road closures from Starkholmes and Riber residents, many alleging they had not received any prior warnings about the long traffic delays.

Not as big as Bakewell Show, but Ashover Show packs them in year after year – and 1967 was no exception. Fine weather helped to swell the crowds but there was always space to stop, chat and eat candy floss.

John Hole, of Eddlestow Hall Farm, Ashover, receiving the Astell Trophy for his prize-winning Short Horn heifer from Mrs G W Astell.

Just like home...members of Ashover Women's Institute busy washing pots to provide cups of tea for visitors.

Father and son, Geoff and David Brailsford, of Honeycroft Farm, Alton, laden with trophies and leading their prize-winning Friesian bull Farley Croft Beau in the grand parade.
Later in the afternoon as Geoff was loading the beast into the cattle truck, it crushed him against the side severely bruising his ribs and breaking his collar bone.

The Gypsy in question was Italian star Franco Nero, seen here on the steps of his caravan on Beeley Moor above Chatsworth House. Franco gained a business degree at Milan University and later studied medicine. He also played Sir Lancelot in '*Camelot*'.

After the filming of '*Women in Love*', 1969 brought yet another D H Lawrence epic to the area for shooting. '*The Virgin and the Gypsy*' visited locations at Beeley Moor, Youlgrave, Cromford, Derwent Dams and Kedleston Hall and many of the extras were drawn from the local population. This shot is of Birchover stone mason Ken Goodwin kitted out as a van driver at Cromford Station.

Joanna Shimkus (Yvette) and Honor Blackman (Mrs Fawcett) at Beely Moor.

When new met old...this diesel car nearly stole the show at Cromford Station and filming was held up while it went about its normal business. Driver of the diesel was Matlock man Bill Hodkin.

Youlgrave local preacher Joe Oldfield appropriately dressed...as a parson.

Tea-break for Youlgrave extras Mrs Pam Parsley, Mrs Lucy Oldfield and Frank Barton.

Honor Blackman (Mrs Fawcett) takes time out for a quick cigarette at Beeley Moor.

Lights, Camera, Action at Beeley Moor.

A quiet day's fishing on the River Wye at Rowsley for Bill Pitts, newly-retired Chief Constable of Derbyshire County Constabulary. Mr Pitts was born at Darley Dale and his father was a Rowsley railwayman.

Secretary of Derbyshire County Council Angling Club, Owen Handley is pictured at Flash Dam inspecting the vegetation and checking water quality. The Club committee were trying to work out ways of reducing the peat level of the water and turning the nine-acre reservoir into a first-class angling site.

Matlock Angling Club member Charlie Prime had the shock of a lifetime in 1962 when he hooked this 22-inch 3lb 14oz rainbow trout on the River Derwent. He was fishing with three maggots on a size 16 hook with a 24oz line.

Would you believe it? Well these men couldn't. Matlock Town Football Club were playing Loughborough on the Causeway Lane Ground in 1962. Early in the game Matlock were awarded a penalty kick which missed its target, and in the second half with the score 1-2, they were awarded another. This time Lambert feebly rolled it at the goal-keeper who gratefully gathered it up – much to the dismay of the spectators who just happened to be: Matlock manager Mick Betteridge, player Gordon Duggins, captain Ian Swift, player Mick Dagley, club secretary George Davis and committee member David Maskrey. The final score was Matlock Town 3, Loughborough 4.

A knock on Peter Vardy's door on the last Friday night in 1967 almost left him speechless. Peter, goalkeeper for local amateur team Rowsley was looking forward to the following day's game with his friends but the man who knocked on the door was Ian Swift, manager of Matlock Town. "You're playing for us against Long Eaton United instead, and we'll see you at Causeway Lane early tomorrow," he said. Before the match Peter was taken on to the pitch by the manager and given plenty of goal-keeping practice that obviously stood him in good stead as he kept a clean sheet in Matlock's 1-0 victory.

What a difference 18 months make...as Peter Vardy found out. Despite a poor show against Ashby when Matlock were defeated in the last fixture of the season, Peter found the criticisms of his keeping that day hard to take. However, despite that, the team travelled to Gainsborough the following week and when they arrived at the ground they learned they had won the League championship. "Everyone went crazy," said Peter, "and I went out feeling right on top of everything." But disaster followed and he broke his right arm in the first save of the match.

Patiently waiting for the signal to change – and ultimately change their lives – are past fireman Bill Hodkin and driver Walter Else. Within a few minutes of this picture being taken they would be making a historic journey in Class 8 loco No 48214 – that of being the last steam-driven freight train ever to leave Northwood Sidings.

Amid a cloud of steam and smoke, engine No 48214 leaves Northwood on October 1st, 1966, on its final journey for Garston loaded with coal.

Already buildings and track are being demolished, but engines and men are still working as the sidings near closure.

To the south of Northwood, shunters move wagons and materials as the great shut down gets under way...

...while to the north is a scene of dereliction. Empty, weed-filled lines which, during the Second World War, were regularly crammed full of rolling stock carrying guns, tanks, lorries and all the paraphernalia of war. In peaceful times the lines carried milk from the Express Dairy at Rowsley, stone from local quarries and, of course, coal, not to mention the passenger link to Manchester and the north in general.

No-one could deny that working on the railways was easy, but between their shift patterns the men managed to find time to look after their allotments, gardens, pigeons, and under the guidance of Jack Smedley ran a very popular concert party and cricket team. Jack is seen here (front seated) with Mrs Doxey, Doug Gannicott and June Gannicott performing one of their hilarious sketches.

Jack Smedley donned his wicket keeper's pads when the Loco and Traffic teams met in their annual charity match at Rowsley in 1961. Proceeds of £60 from this match and a community sing song afterwards went to four colleagues who had been off work for six months. Unfortunately Jack was on the losing side and Loco won by 76 runs to retain the Collie Cup. Among those pictured are Jack, Charlie Gratton, Fred Kenworthy, Dennis Plant, George Seedhouse, 'Sned' Gilbert, Tom Ambrey, L Flint, Harold Grimshaw, Harold Wall, Ted Harper, Frank Lowe and Dennis Lane.

Rowsley Branch of the National Union of Railwaymen was always an active organisation, holding regular meetings and looking after its members. Pictured here in 1961 is Mr David Taylor, an engine driver for 30 years, receiving a £50 Benevolent Fund cheque from Councillor Jack Turner (branch secretary). With them are Luke Hopkinson, Bill Horobin (Matlock Urban District Council chairman and also a railwayman), Mr W Charlton, Mr S Gratton and NUR representative Mr Corbett.

Although the line north of Matlock was closed, the W H Smith bookstall remained open under the watchful eye of Bryan Crapper. He was appointed manager in 1954 and is seen here serving customers in 1967, just one year before becoming proprietor. The following year he moved the business to Crown Square, eventually retiring in 1988.

Railway pensioners and their wives were always taken care of and one of the highlights was the annual outing – by train of course, and organised by members of the Rowsley Retired Railwaymen's Association. Here they are in July 1960, gathered on Darley Dale station waiting to go to Blackpool not by steam engine but a diesel loco. One hundred and eighty-six passengers boarded the train but when it was time to return three ladies were missing. They eventually caught another train to Buxton and then on to Matlock by taxi. There are many familiar faces in this picture, but only a few of their names come to mind: Mr and Mrs George Burton, Mr and Mrs Jack Donalin, George Paulson, Mrs Hudson, Mr and Mrs Harold Barnes, Cyril Pearson, Sid Burgess, Arthur Wilson and his son, Tom Walters, Jack Smedley senr., Mr and Mrs Harry Slaney, Frank Watts, Alf Grafton, Dennis Plant, Mr and Mrs Edgar Hallows, Mr and Mrs Bill Stone, Mr and Mrs Jim Thompson, Mr and Mrs Sid Smedley, Mrs Hill and Mr and Mrs Sam Morton.

High Peak Junction was between Cromford and Whatstandwell and linked the main line railway with Buxton. As well as passengers in the early days it also hauled freight and collected milk from farms as it wound its way across the Peak towards Buxton. The trucks were hauled by steam power and cable up the steep inclines and then attached to engines to continue on their way. On the way down to the Junction the line split and went either side of a catch pit that was brought into operation should there be a run-away. This picture taken in the early '60s shows the split and on closer inspection an upturned wagon protruding out of the top of the pit.

This shows just how effective the catch pit was and is now well worth a visit as recent excavations have revealed a wagon still embedded in it.

Rowsley Station is abandoned, uncared for and weed-filled. It was once the stopping-off point for Royalty and day-trippers to Chatsworth House and the starting point for thousands of gallons of milk bound for London from the nearby Express Dairy. It was eventually dismantled with a view to being re-built at Peak Rail's Buxton depot. Before that could happen half the stone was stolen and the remainder used to build a toilet block at Darley Dale Station after Peak Rail left Buxton for Rowsley. The wrought iron canopies with their glass panels were designed by Sir Joseph Paxton.

As the main line north out of Matlock was axed so was the Cromford and High Peak railway. The Matlock Mercury under the guidance of owner-editor Ella Smith and her reporters wrote copious words, MPs pledged their support, petitions were signed but there was nothing which could be done – Dr Beeching's axe had fallen and hundreds of people were out of work. Here Mrs Smith interviews railwaymen at Homesford Cottage as they prepare to say farewell to the shunting engines that had served them so well. They include Frank Jackson, 'Tiger' Hadfield, Ron Eley, "Ginger" Turner and Roy Wain.

All packed up and nowhere to go...the Saddle Tankers from High Peak prepare to leave on their final journey. Note the number (47000) of the front engine. Some five years earlier this was involved in a nasty mishap at the top of the Sheep Pasture Incline (see picture below). It was repaired and went into service again.

Here is Saddle Tank No 47000, upside down at the top of Sheep Pasture Incline. Once removed and refurbished, it was soon back in service.

It wasn't only steam engines that had accidents. In 1969 this 136-ton diesel loco, hauling 27 wagons of Derbyshire stone, was derailed near Wirksworth Station while on its way to Derby. Driver George Chadwick was unhurt.

Crowds gathered on the Hopton Incline in 1967 to watch and photograph a nostalgic moment when Saddle Tank No 68012, hired by the Stephenson Loco Society and driven by George Repton, made a last trip on the Cromford and High Peak Railway line.

When John Hall, Station Master at Wirksworth retired in 1963, he was replaced by two men – one in charge of operations and the other on the commercial side. Although passenger trains ceased in 1947, he was still responsible for the freight traffic that ran from the town's quarries. Mr Hall was keenly interested in all things relating to Wirksworth, being a founder member and president of the Rotary Club. At various times he was chairman, secretary and treasurer of the Well Dressings committee. He was also Cub Master and secretary of the Scouts Association.

Bill Rosling, was Station Master at Matlock Bath from 1947 to 1966 from where he retired after 47 years railway service. He began his railway career as a 13-year-old junior clerk at Matlock Station, later becoming Station Master at Whittingon (Chesterfield) and Bescot Junction (Walsall). As well as railway duties, he was also an ardent worker for the Matlock Bath Venetian Fete, helping to revive it after the war. Mr Rosling played a major role in arranging the extra trains that brought thousands of visitors flocking to the town for the Fete and Illuminations. He was also a member of the Attractions Committee and is pictured by the side of one of the tableaux.

The last steam engine to pass through Matlock Station in June 1968, was this special carrying the name plates 'Oliver Cromwell'. The engine had previously stopped at Derby Station while the wooden name plates were fitted before its journey continued northwards.

The district was shocked to learn in June, 1969, that popular market trader Billy Clay had been killed in an accident at several places in the county - but no-one was more shocked than the man himself. "Letters of condolence have been sent to my wife and even the insurance man called round" quipped a far-from-dead Billy, alive and kicking as he gave his famous moustache an extra twirl while serving customers at his Matlock stall.

Taken in 1968 this aerial shot of Matlock shows many 'relics' of the recent past: the bowling green outside the Town Hall; the open-air Lido; open-air market; the then-new bus station that was later demolished to make way for a supermarket as was the market; the fairground behind Spa Villas; the rear of Woolworths before the land was developed... and more eye-catching, the railway activity in the station area. Although the line was closed to passenger services there are still wagons of limestone to be seen running into the Derbyshire Stone site and into the parcels and goods depot at the side and rear of the station.

Peregrine, Lord Hartington's Coming of Age Ball at Chatsworth House saw a special train load of guests arriving at Matlock Station in 1965. Among them were Princess Margaret, seen here with her Lady in Waiting Lady Elizabeth Cavendish and Lord Snowdon. They are being escorted down the steps by Station Master Alan Fletcher.

After nine years of bad weather for the annual South Peak Junior Schools swimming gala, fortunes changed in 1967. The sun came out at Matlock Lido and winners of the small schools (with less than 100 pupils) section were Matlock Town, while the large school champions were Matlock All Saints. The Town team pictured with their trophy are Alison MacPherson, Helen Roe, Terence Gratton, Tony Morris (all aged 11), Louise Parsons and Tina Flint (aged 10). Also in the picture is Bill Bowler who later became Head of the John Turner School in Darley Dale.

January, 1969, saw the district almost at a standstill with snow and freezing temperatures. Here Matlock Lido superintendent Jack Soppitt tries to bring a touch of humour to the situation. With the small indoor pool drained for maintenance he contemplated opening the main outdoor pool, which had a two-inch thick covering of ice...for skating?

Pictured on their pitch at Cromford Meadows are the Old Bailean RUFC 1st XV team. They include (left to right, back row): Sid Quigley, Dave Ramsden, Mike Thornton, Terry Boswell, Wally Redfern, Gerald Newton, Bill Walton (front row) Ian Stuart, John Siddall, John Billingham (captain), Mick Marsden, John Lowry and Malcolm Macfadyen.

A trio of Old Bailean rugby players whose service to the club added up to nearly 70 years. On the left are John Hooton (36), second team prop forward and match secretary with 20 years service. Centre is Haydn Kingman (44), honorary life member and ex-secretary, and third team hooker with 28 years service. Right is Sid Quigley, vice-chairman, third team prop who had been with the club over 20 years.

Matlock Invitation South Road Federation's first annual dinner was held in 1962, at the Fishpond Hotel in Matlock Bath when pigeon fanciers from all over Derbyshire attended. Guest of honour was Herbert Beetham, the English billiards champion, pictured sitting beside Mrs Ella Smith, owner/editor of the Matlock Mercury and president of the Federation. Other guests pictured include Mr and Mrs Roy Phillips, Mr and Mrs Lewis Blackburn, Mr Fred Holmes (chairman), Mr Len Evans, Mr and Mrs Dennis Lane, Mr Dennis Gregory, Mr Adrian Duggins, Mrs Florence Glew, Mrs Lucy Duggins, Mr Roy Furniss, Miss Susan Jarrett and Mr Harold Hardy.

Bonsall pigeon racing champion Len Gratton won the W E Ridge Rochefort Trophy in Matlock Invitation South Road Federation's 1962 season. He is pictured (second from right) receiving it from Mr G Wilkinson at the annual dinner. Also pictured are Mr and Mrs T Grace, Mr A Baker, Fred Holmes (chairman) and Dennis Gregory (secretary).

More pigeon fliers – this time the Two Dales Invitation Flying Club pictured at their 1962 prize presentation and supper at the Holly Bush Inn, Hackney. Premier trophy winner was Graham Brookhouse (centre) seen receiving the Combined Average Cup from George Wheeldon. Other winners were Dennis Gregory, Eric Evans, Wilf Ridge, Adrian Duggins, Fred Treloar, Len Evans and Ted Gill.

The Duchess of Devonshire spending quality time in 1968 with her daughter Lady Sophia and grandchildren Isabel and Eddie Tennant in the West Front Garden at Chatsworth House.

A flying visit to Chatsworth House and Edensor for Bobbie and Ethel Kennedy in 1964. The Duchess of Devonshire and her daughter Lady Sophia were there to greet them as they stepped from their helicopter.

A regular visitor to Chatsworth House was the Rt. Honourable Harold Macmillan, seen here with the Duke and Duchess of Devonshire and their son Peregrine, Lord Hartington.

Lady Sophia Cavendish, on her Shetland pony Chatsworth Caroline, and the Duchess of Devonshire with her whippet Johnny are almost dwarfed by the size of this jump near the Golden Gates as they look forward to the Chatsworth Horse Trials, 1964.

The sun shone as ATV's Pat Astley crowned Linda Flint as Wirksworth Carnival Queen in 1965. Her attendants were R Hardy, V Wood, S Wall, A Beresford, L Ford and D Moore, with Stephen Phillips and Stephen Moore as pageboys.

The 1967 well dressing festival at Bonsall will go down in history as the year when the Rector, the Revd Lawrence Wood, refused to bless one of the wells. When asked why, he replied: "Well it's wet" and when pressed he later said "We have our reasons." But all was not lost for local Baptist lay preacher Mr George Carline stepped into the breach and is pictured blessing the well.

Smiling again after the well she designed had finally been blessed is Mrs Sandra Bunting.

Mrs Peggy Blodwell took a flight from Tripoli to design this well in Bonsall entitled Pursuit from Egypt. She had made the journey back to design the well for the previous four years.

Harry Gill, renowned local photographer on the other end of a camera lens proudly displays an old £5 note. Not just an ordinary note, but one which served as an autograph book and on which many famous names were written. Among them were England Manager Alf Ramsay and players Jimmy Greaves, Bobby Moore, Roger Byrne and Gordon Milne, all collected while the team were training at Lea Green sports centre.

Matlock character Joe Woodhouse once had his pocket picked — by an elephant — while visiting Billy Smart's Circus in Chesterfield. A confirmed bachelor, Joe (pictured here in 1967) lived with his mother in the cottage where he was born. After she died from burns sustained in a fire, he joined a matrimonial agency at the age of 60, met and married Dorothy and they had ten happy years together before she died. After that he spent his time reading, wandering the town or just sitting with his dog Judy on the steps at the gate of his little cottage in Lumsdale, which was his home for nearly 80 years.

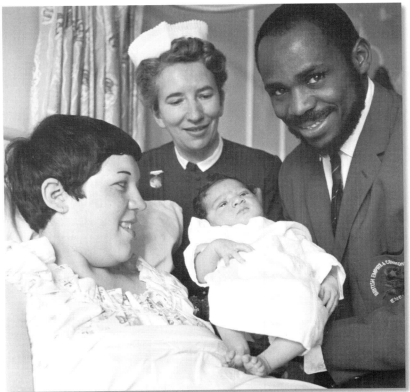

When Olympic silver medallist Louis Martin accepted an invitation to open a garden party at Wirksworth Maternity Hospital in July, 1967, little did he know his wife Ann would be in there at the same time having their first child. The garden party was on the Saturday and baby Louis Paul was born the following day when Louis senior brought along his medal that he had won for weight lifting at the Tokyo Olympics. Pictured with the trio is Matron Miss J R H Southam.

Thanks to the inclusion of four 'guest' players, David Horobin, Jim McCann, Barry White and Alan Barnes, Matlock Wanderers beat their rivals Matlock Rovers by 4 goals to 2 on the Farley Hill ground in December 1961. Horobin opened the scoring, McCann added another goal, and White then netted twice. Towards the end Rovers struck back and Roddy Johnson scored two. Pictured (top) are Matlock Rovers: (back row) Peter Soppitt, Bob Price, Geoff Treloar, Alan Allwood, Alistair Dawson, Stuart Fearn; (front row) Roddy Johnson, Mick Wiltshire, Ernie Dance (captain), Ivan Hardy and 'Tant' Smith. Matlock Wanderers (bottom picture), back row: (left to right) Keith Blair, Jim McCann, David Horobin, Louis Bean, John Taylor, John Bateman and Rowland Harris; front row: Michael Wheeldon, Graham Barnes, Barry White, Garry Sladin and Ernest Briddon.

While climbing Yokecliffe Rocks two youngsters from Wirksworth got into difficulties and were rescued by Matlock firemen. David Dickenson (12) and Jane Phillips (11) reached a ledge 30 feet from the ground but then realised they were stranded. David's sister saw their plight and ran to a phone to get help. A fireman was lowered to the ledge and the children were hauled up to safety before being whisked away to their home, none the worse for their adventure.

With Matlock Bath Illuminations moving further down the River Derwent the need for a temporary bridge lower down was necessary to cope with the visitors that were expected. Scaffolding (Great Britain) Ltd are seen here erecting the 130-foot long structure that was five feet wide.

Walter Bird as caretaker of Matlock Urban District Council's Grand Pavilion, was also in charge of their rowing boats which could be hired from the landing stage. He's pictured at the helm of the motor boat used to 'rescue' the odd rower who went too close to Masson Weir.

In 1967 Jack Woodhouse was awarded the British Empire Medal for his services to the gas industry. Like the gas holder in the background Mr Woodhouse is now gone, but the work he was responsible for is still serving the district. He was in charge of the scheme to lay the gas linking main over High Tor and fitting the boosters up the slope. He was also in charge of laying the new main from Matlock to Sheffield, via Chatsworth and Baslow.

A historic day in the sorting office at Matlock Post Office for Geoff Marsden, Trevor Toplis, Davis Hodgkinson and Don Smith as they hand-sort for the last time some of the thousands of letters which they handled. It was in 1967 that post codes came into use and thereby eased their work load.

Harold Bradbury was a man who loved his work as a taxi proprietor and he was still driving in 1968 at the ripe old age of 80. His business was based on Smedley Street and he recalled how he regularly worked seven days and sometimes through the night, driving the local midwife out on calls. He claimed babies usually held on until late at night before being born!

In the 1960s October saw the start of the 'season' for climbing High Tor, and in 1961 Graham West and his companion Graham Baxter were the first to scale the limestone cliff. After six hours toil Graham reached the summit only to be faced by warden Arthur Thorpe demanding 6d admission fee to the grounds. Graham argued that his feet were still over the edge so that didn't count.

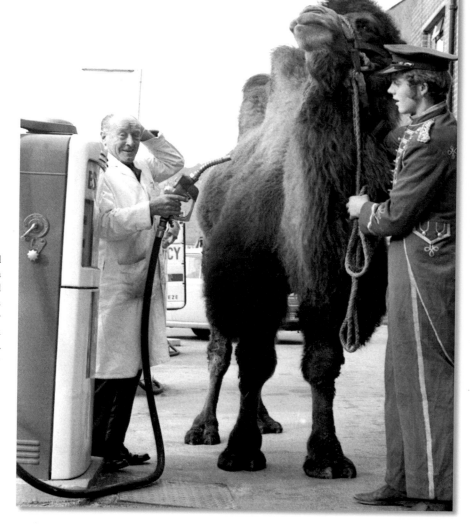

"Fill him up" said the man with a camel as he called in to Platts Motors Garage on Causeway Lane in Matlock one day in 1968. "Sure," said attendant George Jepson, "how much and where does he want it?" It turned out it was water he wanted not petrol, and after several gallons Achmed happily returned to the circus with his tanks full.

Members of Matlock Inner Wheel celebrated their 16th Charter anniversary in 1962 at the New Bath Hotel. Guest speaker was Mr A B Cruikshank, warden of the newly-opened Matlock Adult Education Centre which was later named Tawney House. Among those pictured are Mrs D Allen (secretary), Mrs G Rhodes, Mrs N Grey, Mrs W K Wheatcroft (president), Mrs M E Grant (treasurer) and Mrs W A Horner (vice-president).

Above: Youngest competitor in the 1962 Matlock and District Young Farmers Club dry stone walling competition at Littlemoor Farm, Riber, was 15-year-old Stuart Hole, of Wayside Farm, Matlock Moor. Pictured third from the left, Stuart was taking part in his first-ever contest and took second place. Working alongside him are John Hayes (Rowsley), Harry Walker (Wakebridge) and Peter Wells (Bow Wood, Lea).

Righ: Joe Neville of Tansley pictured in his early days of shooting. He later went on to become an internationally renowned shot and is currently manager of the England team.

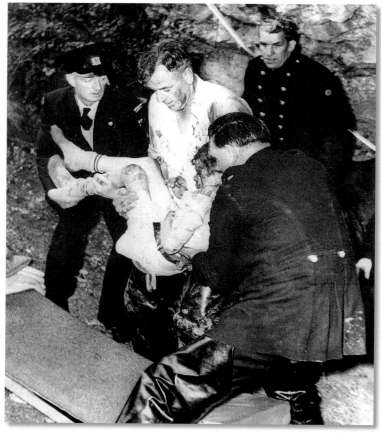

Lucky to be alive was how rescuers described a Boy Scout's escape from death after he had fallen down a shaft at Ball Eye Mine in Bonsall. Firemen and ambulance men from Matlock spent three hours underground before they could bring 11-year-old David Payne to the surface. He is seen here in the arms of Fireman Ray Hurst and aided by Fireman Frank Teece. Only days earlier an experienced pot-holer had died from injuries he received when he fell down the same mine. Playing a major role in that incident was 23-year-old Jonathon Tye (pictured at the scene), who went to assist after hearing there had been an accident. After firemen had managed to get a hoist round the injured Derby man he became wedged under an overhang, so Mr Tye climbed down a rope ladder and with the help of Police Constable Doug Bamforth managed to free the limp body of the 15-stone pot-holer.

Secretary Peggy Davies was the hero of the day when Steetley Refractory Brick Co. Ltd's offices were destroyed by fire. As the building burned around her she stayed on the phone long enough to direct the Fire Services to the scene on the moors above Brassington.

Left, below & page 50: Ashton's Bakery at the junction of Smedley Street and Far Green, Matlock, is no more. The Victorian corner shop and house were pulled down to make room for modern houses, but to the older generation Mr and Mrs Ashton are fondly remembered, particularly for allowing them to use their bread oven at Christmas for roasting their turkeys. Mrs Ashton was always busy in her tiny shop by the roadside, while Joe's bakery was at the rear.

A plea for help to the Rt Hon George Brown from Fred Slater, former conductor and secretary of Matlock Band. The band was playing at Dethick, Lea and Holloway carnival while George, MP for Belper, was the guest of honour who performed the opening ceremony. With Bandmaster John Slater (centre) they are looking at plans of the band's new rehearsal room which they believed had been hit by planners unreasonable restrictions on practice hours.

For services rendered, after many years as its secretary, Frank Lowe (third from right) received a farewell gift from colleagues in the Matlock Branch of the Grenadier Guards Comrades Association. Mr Lowe was also a long-serving railway policeman. His wife Dorothy is on the right. Police Sergeant George Venables is on the left.

Farmer and TV personality Ted Moult officially opened Bolehill and Steeple Grange playing fields and afterwards tried his musical skill on Wirksworth Bandmaster Frank Gratton's trombone. Also pictured is Mrs Gill Jordan, the playing field's fund secretary.

The end of a long journey for this 63-year-old tram, built in 1905 – but the start of a whole new career. It is seen arriving at Crich Tramway Museum Society just in time for the 1968 Grand Extravaganza, but up to that moment it was touch and go that it would ever reach there. A gift from the Czech tram building industry (CKD-Praha), it departed only hours before the Russians invaded Czechoslovakia. The six men bringing the tram were cut off from their base and families, but decided to continue the journey via Germany and Holland.

The official handshake of welcome and thanks to the Czechs from Society President Chaceley Humpidge as the tram's driving handle was handed over by Dr Frantisek Horak, commercial attaché at the Czech Embassy.

After opening the Extravaganza, Belper MP the Rt Honourable George Brown, donned his driver's cap and took Prague 180 for a "spin".

Radio 'ham' George Briddon had an almost ringside seat at his home in Matlock as he listened in to the dramatic events taking place in Czechoslovakia. The 75-year-old heard from a pirate radio, how resistance units were being set up to try and slow down the Russian invaders. Another told of a Russian fleet patrolling the coast, while yet another claimed he was broadcasting from high up in the mountains. "These contacts were the most interesting I have ever made," said George, "but I shall be monitoring the situation closely from now on."

Welcoming smiles from Carol Stone (14) and Jane Birds (14) as they greet overseas visitors to the 1967 Bakewell Show. Both pupils at the Lady Manners School and both from Youlgrave, they thoroughly enjoyed meeting foreign visitors who came from all over Europe and the USA.

Derbyshire Young Farmers clubs staged a "Farming Through the Ages" exhibition and this traction engine and harvester led the procession.

Matlock Round Table found a novel way of advertising their charity stall at the show with these bikini-clad young ladies. Sisters Joan and Angela Noble flank former Miss Matlock and later top model Barbara Dick as they show off the two main prizes – a double bed and a motorised bicycle.

While the sun shone youngsters busied themselves building sand castles in the children's corner.

...but a couple of hours later there was a tremendous thunderstorm which rapidly brought an end to what had been a lovely day... although not everyone was in a rush to finish their ice cream.

Taking centre stage were the High Peak Hunt hounds under the watchful eye of the Master.

Another centre ring attraction was trotting and among the competitors was Matlock's Derek James with Little Eva.

It took only five hours to erect this 'single Bailey bridge' over the River Wye just in time for the 1968 Bakewell Show. Soldiers from the 106 West Riding Field Squadron Royal Engineers performed the operation.

Austrian Eva Ruber Staier visited Bakewell Show in 1969 in her capacity as Miss World. She is watching top show jumper Ted Edgar, seen reflected in her sunglasses. She later appeared in three James Bond films.

Below: After nearly 40 years behind a desk, teacher Eric Stevens finally called it a day at All Saints' School in Matlock. He arrived there in 1929 and during that time taught three generations of some families. When he was not teaching he was a member of Matlock Urban District Council for many years and was elected chairman in 1962. He became an MBE in the 1962 Birthday Honours List.

All smiles as these ladies try out their new switchboard in new surroundings at Derbyshire County Council Offices in Matlock. Supervisor Joan Revill is at the top of the picture with Audrey Kirk, Margaret Beresford, Iris Woodhouse, Audrey Hobart and June Parker.

Herbert Ankers got a nasty shock when he was working in his neighbour's garden...a hole appeared underneath him and he fell into it. "I thought it was a mine-shaft and that I was about to disappear underground," said the 67-year-old of Holt Drive, Hooley Estate. Fortunately he only went in up to his waist and he was soon "rescued". Council officials thought it was caused by surface water scouring out of a small cavern.

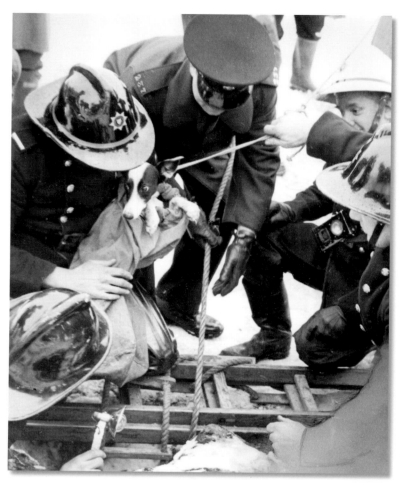

An underground ordeal ended for a Lurcher dog when she was rescued by caving expert Doug Fearn. Fly had been out walking over Winster Moor with his owner Mr Thomas Nutt when they spooked a rabbit. The dog took chase but fell down a mine shaft that was covered with snow. There was no sound from down below and Fly was thought to be dead but the family went back the next day to check. They heard a faint barking from the shaft and quickly alerted the relevant services – Fire Brigade, Police, RSPCA and Cave Rescue. The Press arrived in full force to record the rescue and were there in time to see Matlock' Doug Fearn descend into the depths and send Fly to the surface in a bag to be reunited with 16-year-old David Nutt whose special pet she was. It was only later as the ropes and ladders were being collected that it was realised that Mr Fearn was still in the shaft.

Deep under the hilltops of Middleton-by-Wirksworth there is a mine – not for gold, silver or lead – but for stone. The roadways are enormous, double-deck buses could pass side by side, there is lighting, traffic lights and it is dry. This extra-large tractor is tipping high quality limestone into the crusher before being taken by conveyor to the outside for further processing. Now all is quiet for it closed about a year ago.

Looking back and up towards the crusher and the beginning of the conveyor belt.

Below: At the age of 21, Elton motor cyclist Mick Andrews was asked by Spanish company Ossa to design and develop a machine that would serve as a trials and scrambles bike. After only 18 months it was completed and Mick was under contract and about to ride the machine in the International Six-day Trial in Poland.

In 1964 the Royal Antediluvian Order of Oddfellows Lathkill Lodge No 1004 celebrated sixty years since their inauguration with a dinner at the George Hotel in Youlgrave. Chief guest was the Grand Primo of England Harold Desforges and pictured with him are Albert Shimwell, Herbert Wheeldon, George Crisp, Arnold Oldfield, Albert Prime, Percy Noton, Tom Cassells, George Roper, Hugh Moss, Eric Billinge, Tom Housley, James Rowland, Bernard Hambleton, Clarence Frost and Harold Shimwell.

The Star Club in Hamburg was the Mecca of all music groups in the 60s. The Beatles, Cream, Jerry Lee Lewis and Jimmy Hendrix played there. Matlock's own music outfit – The Sabres, with Derek Townsend on drums, Frank Wyse, Timmy Clay bass guitar, Pete Blatherwick rhythm guitar, Richard Bateman lead guitar and Bob Price vocals played there after an audition in Liverpool. They appeared at the Star Club for three weeks, but despite being offered a further contract, the lads packed their bags and headed home.

Fire ravaged Cromford Colour works and while no-one was severely injured, the damage caused was substantial. Eventually the business closed and the buildings now form part of the historic Cromford Arkwright Mill complex.

Work under way on Matlock's new Police Station on Bank Road opposite the town Hall. Buildings were demolished to make way for the project, and some of the stone removed was used to build a house off Asker Lane. The lower part of the Police Station was kept intact, the semi-detached Police houses in the background were demolished and now form part of the vehicle park off Lime Grove Walk.

Floods in Matlock are nothing new, but in 1965 and 1968 two were particularly severe. One man died, a car was 'parked' up a tree and thousands of pounds of damage was caused to businesses and homes.

John Turner School pupils sit this one out at Four Lanes End, Darley Dale.

The Horse Shoe public house at the junction of Chesterfield Road and Causeway Lane, Matlock Green.

Clearing up the aftermath in the basement warehouse of Marsdens grocery shop on Matlock Green.

All aboard...Derbyshire Stone Ltd laid on huge lorries to ferry workers around the town.

Outside the Matlock Mercury offices, Bakewell Road, looking towards Crown Square.

Meanwhile inside the Mercury offices Neville Boulton, Terence Stone, Jack Mudway and Adrian Duggins stand waist-deep in filthy, smelly water as they try to salvage the week's edition.

...which they did under the guidance of Editor Gerry Kreibich. Twenty pages were condensed to twelve, but as the type-setting machines were out of action because there was no electricity and they were under three feet of water, the front page had to be set by hand.

The Christmas lights in Crown Square look pretty as the water begins to back-up at around 7 pm.

Taken around midnight, the decorations cast a surreal light as a bus is stranded at the entrance to Bank Road, the water rushes through Crown Square, along Causeway Lane, into Firs Parade and on towards the football ground.

The bleak scene looking from Stanton Moor. Darley Bridge is to the right and in the hazy distance Riber Hillside.

For years Cromford Tors had been the source of much frustration to drivers as they waited patiently to negotiate the narrow twisting bottleneck. This picture was taken in 1960 just before work began on the widening scheme, which involved the demolition of the Glenorchy Chapel, cottages, a public house and hundreds of tons of limestone as well as re-aligning the A6 northwards.

The work in progress in 1961: forget health and safety as schoolboys gathered to get a closer look.

Blasting the rock away

One way of removing stubborn rock...
by bulldozer and a long rope.

Drilling holes in the massive fallen boulders
ready for them to be reduced to a more
manageable size.

As a sequel to the A6 road widening at Cromford in 1961 and subsequently at Matlock Bath in 1968 the County Council erected signs at Cromford advising motorists "Buxton Avoiding Matlock" and re-routing them up the Via Gellia, and at Picory Corner "Derby Avoiding Matlock". Matlock UDC Councillor Remo Tinti and Chamber of Trade members took exception to this and created a political storm by removing the signs early one morning and delivering them back to the County Council depot. Here Councillor Tinti, Chamber secretary Bob Mitchell and amusement arcade owner Harry Hall are pictured at Cromford on the first phase of their mission.

On to Picory Corner, the second phase completed with Councillor Tinti carrying the Derby sign, followed by Bob Mitchell with portable steps, and Derbyshire Times reporter Sam Fay and Matlock Mercury reporter Adrian Tame hanging on to their every word.

The evening after Olga Terenczyn was chosen as Miss Winster 1968 she was involved in a vehicle accident and spent three days in hospital. Olga (17), of East Bank, Winster, and a trainee cook at Nottingham University, was knocked unconscious in the crash in Nottingham and had ten stitches in her face, and cuts and bruising to her head, legs and arms.

Tansley Brunswick Chapel on Nottingham Road was due to be demolished in September, 1963, but when the workmen arrived on the first day they discovered the building had collapsed during the night.

Sunday, January 9, 1966 just before lunch. A scene of devastation as one of the pair (Nos. 3 and 4) are demolished in minutes by an enormous landslip from the quarry behind. The houses were occupied at the time, but all the residents got out without injury. Nos. 1 and 2 had to be demolished later because of the unstable condition of the ground and quarry. Living in No 1 were the Edwards family, No 2 the Knapps, No 3 the Wilkinsons and No 4 the Bothams.

Roof timbers balance precariously over the road as traffic goes by.

Higher up the quarry slope workmen drill massive boulders, some estimated at weighing over 200 tons, before they were safely dynamited.

A climber on the face of High Tor, down below the river, the A6 and on the other side the pair of semi-detached houses Nos. 1, 2, 3 and 4 Hazel Bank

An excited Beverley Crowder shows off her Queen's Guide certificate to other members of the Matlock All Saints' Guide Company – Kay Storey, Christine Winnard, Gillian Hall and Janet Holden.

Leading cyclists from all over the Midlands took part in Winster Carnival's 20-mile road race round the village in 1969. Winner of the 10-lap event up the steep banks and through the narrow streets was Matlock Cycling Club's Ken Wilson, with team-mate Eric Stone one minute 12 seconds adrift. Carnival Queen Stephanie Roose presented Ken with the winner's medal – and a kiss.

Thousands of pounds were spent in 1965 on Rowsley Bridge being virtually re-built despite being only a matter of months before the rail link north of Matlock was axed by Dr Beeching. The low, narrow arch was taken down and replaced by a girder span so allowing larger vehicles to pass safely under. This picture is the 'new look' bridge taken from the Bakewell side.

...while this shows the profile of the old bridge from the Matlock side before it, too, was altered. When the railway line was eventually closed in 1968, the new bridge was demolished in the interests of road safety.

A lucky escape for the driver of this mobile cement mixer when he lost control down Steep Turnpike, Matlock. It crossed Causeway Lane, crashed through the bushes and narrowly missed the toilet block in the Hall Leys Park before overturning.

Another narrow escape – this time on Lea Bottom. The driver was trapped upside down with his head only inches from the river, his lorry held precariously in trees on the bank. Fireman Joe Harsthorne worked waist-high in water as he disconnected the battery while spilled fuel leaked on to it. The driver was not seriously injured.

Sydnope Hill, Two Dales, 1968. The driver of this lorry escaped serious injury after he and his vehicle had survived crashing through a wall and falling 80 feet into a ditch where it jack-knifed after impact. Albert Fletcher, Graham Brookhouse and Mrs Betty Wood, all of whom lived nearby, were first on the scene and they helped release the driver who was sitting in the passenger seat with the steering wheel jammed into the back of the driver's seat.

Yet another crash on Sydnope Hill – this time a fatal one. Loaded with animal feed, the lorry overturned just before the first bend spilling half of the load. The driver apparently tried to jump clear but his sleeve caught in the door and he was trapped under the side of the vehicle.

A workman was trapped in his van for over 30 minutes after it slid into a 10-foot deep trench at Holloway. He had tried to get out of the vehicle before it became stuck but his leg was trapped between the door and the trench side. Matlock Fire Service and workers managed to release him and he was stretchered the 500 yards to an ambulance. As he lay on the stretcher he was asked if he would like a cigarette which he declined, saying that he never smoked in bed. His leg was broken in two places.

Matlock's first cable car? Getting coal to Lyn Willies' home high up on the hillside near Artists' Corner was always a problem, but one which he solved by erecting a 'ski-lift'. The bags of coal were tipped into a container which was then winched up the steep slope. Mining expert Dr Willies also used the system to take materials up and down when he re-laid the floors of his house.

Derbyshire Stone Ltd received an order in 1967 for a quarter of a million tons of limestone blocks, some of them weighing eight or nine tons each. Special trains from Middle Peak Quarry, Wirksworth, and Caldon Low Quarry at Buxton were taking the stone to Port Talbot, South Wales, where a new harbour was being built. The contract completion was expected to last between six and 12 months with one train per day making the trip.

Hundreds of youngsters from all over Derbyshire united in a "Youth Against Hunger" march in 1966. They used Matlock, Bakewell or Chesterfield as their starting points but all had to complete the triangular course. Jane McKay, of Hurst Rise, Matlock, raised £51 1s 6p during her epic 32-mile journey accompanied by Patricia Holmes, also of Matlock. Pictured in Baslow are Denise Sammons, Peter Laight, Jane Duggins, Mick Knowles and Jean Siddall.

Having a rollicking time are these members of Matlock High Tor Players who performed 'The Health Service' in the Town Hall as part of their 1963 season. Pictured are Wendy Hepplewhite, Paul Wolfendon and Jack Hammond.

The annual parade of the Derbyshire Fire Services was held at the County Offices in Matlock when Lord Lieutenant Sir Ian Walker-Okeover inspected the firemen and presented them with their medals.

Wilfred Pickles and Mabel were in Birchover in 1963 recording a programme called 'Pleasant Journey'. They are pictured with County Councillor Norman Wilson chatting to Jane Stacey (18) at the wheel of a tractor at Cowclose Farm. They also met and recorded items from quarry worker Gil Housley and blacksmith Bill Clark.

The object 9-year-old Wilfred Bown found near his home at Butterley Farm Cottage, Ashover, caused a great deal of curiosity among the family. Brother John (14) thought their father Dick should examine it, so the object was put on to the kitchen tableand he thought it might be of military origin – until he noticed a pin with three available positions "Safe" "Travel" and "Fire". He immediately ran to the door and hurled it down the field but nothing happened. A call was made to the police who arrived and called the army who in turn called out the bomb disposal squad. The object was found to be a pre-World War I stick grenade that they said should be buried and then exploded. Mr Bown said he didn't like the idea of his cattle eating bits of shrapnel so it was decided to place it in a hollow fallen tree for detonation. The whole family – Dad, Mum, John, Wilfred, Doreen (13), Kathleen (3) and David (2) – gathered at the window to witness the event which split the tree in half. Later they they were told that had the grenade exploded while they were handling it they would certainly have all been killed. All clear and all smiles from Wilfred as he posed happily in front of the tree.

If your surname is Matlock then the obvious thing to do would be to go to the town and see if there are any links – and that is what Julian Clifton Matlock, Jnr. did in 1969. He came from Los Angeles via Sweden where he was working as musical director on a TV series with Ray Conniff and Tony Bennett. 'Buddy's' father, 'Matty' Matlock, is the internationally-known jazz clarinetist, so it's no surprise that 'Buddy' is a singer and guitarist. However no links with Matlock were found but 'Buddy' claimed Matlock folk were the happiest and cheeriest he had ever met.

When Caroline Dale was 23 she became the first woman to carry off the top prize for the way in which she played a selection of coaching calls at the 1967 Royal Show. Caroline was taught to play by her father William, founder of the Red House Stables in Darley Dale.

The winning boat in the 1967 Venetian Fete was this spectacular entry Aqua Magic created by Matlock Bath's own Stuart Wright which featured a spectacular jet of sparkling 'water.'

First prize-winning entry in the 1969 Matlock Bath Venetian Fete was this spectacular fairy castle built by schoolboy Dennis Green (14) who is seen receiving the Arkwright Cup and cash prize from Mrs Bernard Swain.

Keith Howard's entry winning third prize and the Sheffield Wire Rope up was Lunar Module. His young cousins Neil and Andrew Hunt were the astronauts.

Whitworth Institute billiards players won all three Orme Billiards Leagues in the 1964 season. Standing with their trophies are: Malcolm Gadsby, Albert Hand, John Barnes, Philip Saunders, David Pownall, Richard Johnson, George Woodhouse, John Falder, Horace Woodhouse, Jim McCann, Fred Kenworthy and Anthony Smith.

Once a year Youlgrave residents dammed the river in Bradford Dale for an aquatic pillow fight which generally was fun for the winner but left the losers with dampened spirits.

At the age of 19 and showing great promise, Darley Dale's Jim McCann won the Whitworth Institute Trustees Trophy. Over the years which followed he was a regular member of the England team, won the Grand Masters' championship twice, held numerous other titles and won the Derbyshire billiards championship 12 times.

Wensley Football Club pictured on the Causeway Lane ground before one of their cup games are: Back row (left to right) Peter Marshall, Barry Daniels, Peter Lowe, Barry Mackay, Brian Ashbrook and Graham Brookhouse. Front row: Jim McCann, Malcolm White, George Boden, Malcolm Smith and Malcolm Boden.

Left: Fred Kenworthy, George Woodhouse and Jeffrey Jackson clinched the Orme Billiards League 'A' division championship in 1965. Fourth member of the team was Pat Turner.

Below: Matlock Cricket Club was never short of class players in the 60s, one of them, Les Bradbury, claimed ten wickets in one match and later went on to play in League cricket. Back row (left to right): Cliff Russell (chairman), Peter Sellors, Gerald Newton, Dave Ramsden, Brian Cobb, Ian Blackburn, Terry Boswell and Alan Cox (secretary). Front row: Clive Sanders, Keith Leah, Les Bradbury, Gordon Andrews and Harry Hall.

In 1967 several Derbyshire cricketers joined Colonel Peter Hilton's XI for a match against Wirksworth. Among them were Bill Taylor, George Dawkes, Cliff Gladwin and David Baggatt. The home side included Vernon Sandars, Ernest Bunting (umpire), Stan Greatorex, Vincent Vallance, John Thompson, Colin Hopkinson, Ian Chalmers, Ken Wilson, Alan Marples, Graham Buckley, Brian Wanford, Arthur Killer and Richard Needham.

Lea Mills Welfare Football Club ended the 1960–61 season with a 'hat-full' of trophies and are seen here proudly showing off the Ripley and District Youth Cup, Rowsley Invitation Shield and the Ripley League Sportsmen's Cup. Back row: Mr Meikle-Janny, Brian Lee, Mr Hatch, Mr L Clark, Mr H Thompson, Mr S Bartlett and Mr Riley. Middle row: Colin Hopkinson, Robert Burrows, Granville Martin, Paddy Cooke, Lawrence Marchington, David Thompson and Jimmy White. Front row: Andy Bartlett, Glynn Waite, John Taylor, Tony Spencer and George Taylor.

Wirksworth Ivanhoe Football Club, 1961-62. This picture includes E Howard, B Wanford, A Woolley, R Needham, J Linthwaite, W Walton, M Hall, P Brewell, N Lawrence, A Spencer, C Hallows, L Dean, A Bunting; R Jackson, A Bartlett, W Mather, M Hallows, G Bunting, G Slack and R Benyon.

Wirksworth United Football Club, 1963-64. Back row (left to right) G Wanford, C Hopkinson, I Fearn, A Taylor, K Gell, A Marples, G Buckley and secretary Malcolm Hitchcock; front row P Haywood, P Barnett, G Taylor, R Else and W Mather.

Mrs David Brooke-Taylor of the Dower House in Winster crowned Sheila Hodgkinson as the village carnival queen in 1965. Attendants were Maureen Heath, Ruth Vincent, Ann Bacon, Jeanette Robinson and Sandra Tunnicliffe.

Elsie Smedley is pictured being crowned Youlgrave Carnival Queen surrounded by attendants Lorna Bristow, Jill Riley, Jackie Elliott, Heather Blackwell and Jennifer Rose.

Wirksworth Well Dressing Queen in 1964 was Janet Eccleshare seen here being crowned by Mrs Winifred Hilton, of Alton Manor. Janet's speech was written especially for her in Shakespearean-style by family friend Len Yeomans, and was used later by other queens. Her senior attendants were Kathleen Sallis and Sylvia Smart.

A particularly harsh winter in 1963 left officials wondering if there would be a well dressing festival in Wirksworth, but unusually high temperatures in May meant that flowers were in abundance and the festivities went ahead as planned. In glorious sunshine Mrs D G Gilman, of Slaley Hall, crowned Julie Wood as Well Dressings Queen and who was attended by her sister Janet, Susan Clay, Janet Ward, Susan Doxey, Ruth Ward and Sandra Rhodes. Pageboys were Malcolm Andrews and Roger Platts.

Right: Mrs Max Turner crowned 15-year-old Judith Critchlow Queen of Beeley Carnival in 1963. She is seen here with her attendants, Carol Briddon and Judith Harrison, and pageboy Stephen Goodwin.

Left: Four attendants and two pageboys flanked Jane Harvey when crowned by Alderman G N Wilson as Wirksworth Well Dressings Queen in 1969. They were Vivien Rhodes, Kay Bumstead, Angela Kirk, Beverley Rowland, Paul Moxon and Stephen Mottershead.

High on the hillside above Northwood near Rowsley "The Hut" stood deserted for many years. Eventually it was bought by the Girl Guide movement and converted into a meeting place for the youngsters. Equipped with 16 bunks for the Guides and five berths for officers "Pax Tor" was officially opened in July 1961. Performing the opening ceremony was Lady Walker-Okeover, president of the Derbyshire Girl Guide movement, who cut the tape, fixed the name-plate to the door, turned the key to the door and led the way inside. Also pictured are County Commissioner Mrs Wilson and Brownie Christine White, of Matlock, who acted as key bearer. The name Pax Tor was suggested by Lady Baden Powell who saw the work in progress in 1960 and said that she and her husband had formerly lived in a house named Pax Hill.

Darley Dale and Matlock Girl Guides joined forces to enjoy a week's camping in fine weather at Birchover.

Hats, scarves and warm coats for these Senior Citizens at Winster pancake races as they dash down Main Street on Shrove Tuesday in 1963.

Councillor Fred Slater, chairman of Wirksworth Urban District Council, popped in to the Hope and Anchor public house to demolish a mile of pennies which customers had raised during the year. Landlord Horace Ellam and his wife are supervising the event.

Wirksworth annual chrysanthemum show took place in the Town Hall in 1963 and attracted record-breaking exhibits and crowds.

Visitors flocked to Bakewell Town Hall to admire the daffodils in the Horticultural Society's 1963 Spring Flower Show.

Surrounded by a bevy of beauties is Philip Wragg in Youlgrave's annual pantomine. Principal girl (centre) is Heather Taylor while the two principal boys are Mary Witham and Frances Bacon. Entitled Snow Bird, the show was written and produced by Norman Wilson, and ran for three days attracting an audience of over 1500.

Youngsters waiting patiently for their speech day to begin at the Charles White Secondary School at Starkholmes.

Once a year members and friends joined together in Wirksworth Dale Methodist Church for a special service and to have a congregational photograph taken. This picture was taken in the late 60s.

South Normanton beauty Colette Egan took the 1965 title of Miss Derbyshire and is pictured at Matlock Bath Pavilion with other contestants and crown bearer Julie Kreibich.

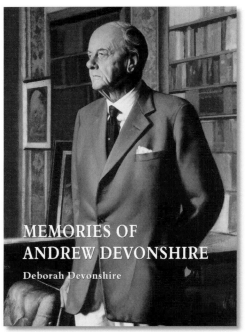
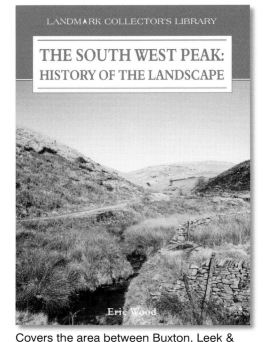
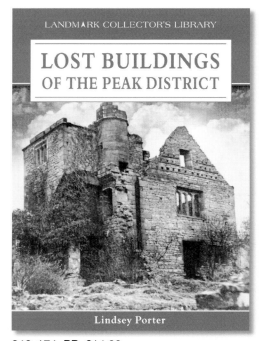
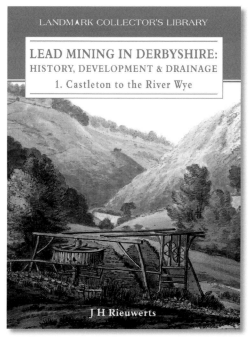